Contents

Acknowledgements

We are very grateful to those who helped us in this project, both in Doncaster and further afield. They include the young women, young men and parents who volunteered to be interviewed and the various individuals, agencies and institutions, who helped us in this task. We would also like to thank the Joseph Rowntree Foundation and the members of the project Advisory Group for their support of the research and contributions, as well as Doncaster Health Authority and colleagues at SATSU.

1 Introduction

Over the last decade teenage pregnancy has been regarded as an increasingly pressing problem for government. This concern has grown with the current administration's focus on socially excluded groups, with teenage mothers being identified as a group with particular, previously unmet, needs. In their report into teenage pregnancy the government's Social Exclusion Unit identified these needs as:

- teenage parents are more likely than their peers to live in poverty and be unemployed

- the death rate for the babies of teenage mothers is 60 per cent higher than that for babies of older mothers

- for half of those under 16 and a third of those aged 16 and 17 teenage pregnancy leads to abortion

- 90 per cent of teenage mothers have their babies outside marriage, and relationships started in the teenage years have at least a 50 per cent chance of breaking down.

These needs might also have consequences for the state through:

- the social costs of teenage pregnancy for the individual, the family and the state

- the wider economic costs in preventing young women from entering the workforce.

In response government has placed teenage pregnancy at the top of its agenda with the publication of the Social Exclusion Unit's *Teenage Pregnancy* report (Social Exclusion Unit, 1999). In this report government pledges to halve the rate of teenage conceptions within ten years through a series of national and local initiatives that aim first, to prevent teenage conceptions and second, to offer support to young mothers themselves to minimise any disadvantage that early motherhood might bring.

This strategy presents teenage pregnancy as a process having two potential stages where state intervention may both be feasible and make an effective difference.

Clearly the first, conception, requires that we focus upon the cultural and individual factors that surround decision making in relation to becoming and remaining sexually active. The second potential stage at which the state may intervene, according to the *Teenage Pregnancy* report (Social Exclusion Unit, 1999), is only after a young woman has given birth.

However, the important intermediate period of decision making related to the active choice to continue with a pregnancy or to have an abortion receives only a brief mention in the Social Exclusion Unit report. This may be partly because we know little about this crucial time of decision making in young women's lives.

Work on 'teenage pregnancy' has generally concentrated on the consequences of continued pregnancies (Phoenix, 1991) for both the teenage mothers and their children. However, very few studies have asked why, once a pregnancy has been conceived, a young woman may choose to continue with it or to terminate it. Where studies have pursued this question, it is often in passing (Moore and Rosenthal, 1993; Burges and Brown, 1995) and/or only with women who have decided to continue with their pregnancies (Phoenix, 1991). In these studies and a more recent exploration of the views of a variety of young people on teenage pregnancy (Health Education Authority, 1999), it was found that anti-abortion feelings were a significant determinant in the decision to continue.

Other studies into teenage sexuality with respect to AIDS, conducted by the Women Risk and AIDS Project (WRAP) (Holland *et al.*, 1990a, 1991; Thomson and Scott, 1991), have identified how heterosexual encounters are constrained by gendered power relations. These constraints may influence not only the construction of sexual identities but also the potential negotiation of safer sex (Thomson and Scott, 1991). Put simply, young women may feel unable to negotiate their sexual encounters to ensure their own safety. This failure to negotiate may occur regardless of the (typically knowledge based) sex education currently delivered. Rather, dominant constructions of ideal teenage femininity may make it difficult for a young woman to be seen to take control of contraception or to say no to sexual advances (Thomson and Scott, 1991; Holland *et al.*, 1991). This has consequences for AIDS education as well as for the more general aspects of school sex education and reproductive choice.

Lack of discussion about an 'intermediate' third potential moment of intervention into teenage pregnancy in the *Teenage Pregnancy* report may also relate to government unwillingness to address the issue of abortion head on. Unlike decision making before conception, where society and government feel there is a need and a social responsibility to intervene, decisions about abortion do not appear to be high on the government's agenda. Where abortion is discussed it is usually within a framework of private individual choice without examining the social context in which

choices are actually made.

We have little information about the degree to which individuals can or do make a 'choice' regarding abortion. Availability of information about abortion, the variety of provision of services around the country (Abortion Law Reform Association, 1997), the nature of social pressures and values and the short time to decide may severely constrain the options available. In particular we have almost no understanding of the specific constraints on very young women and how these may influence the decision-making process.

The research reported here explores teenage pregnancy and associated reproductive decision making in the context of these wider debates about reproductive choice. Whilst conducted over a similar timeframe to the government's report, this research was commissioned independently. Where appropriate we engage with the *Teenage Pregnancy* report, but our aim is not merely to respond to the issues raised, but rather to examine the reality of choice in young women's lives and the factors that shape any decisions made. The research focuses in particular on the intermediate period of decision making when the teenager has to decide whether to continue with (and so consider the options of parenting or adoption), or terminate her pregnancy.

The fieldwork for the project was undertaken in Doncaster, chosen because of its high levels of teenage pregnancy in a context of broad social deprivation. The research set out to examine the complex factors that shape decisions, reflecting patterns of interaction, social beliefs, attitudes towards parenting, adulthood and sexuality, and formal sources of advice and counselling. In doing this the project explores further the issues raised by the WRAP group in respect of the negotiation of sex at a time of transition from childhood to adulthood (Holland *et al.*, 1991; Thomson and Scott, 1991) within a western culture where, paradoxically, dependency on the family has extended later into adulthood (Jones, 1995), while the age of first sexual encounter has declined.

Moreover, by looking at the realities of 'choice' at this time of transition, the project will interrogate the findings of research where teenage motherhood has been cited as a possible route to independent living and by implication adulthood. Although other research (Burges and Brown, 1995) has disputed this, arguing that in practice a baby may not be a route to independence from the family home because social housing may not be available, or the pregnant teenager may prefer to continue to rely on the support of her family (Phoenix, 1991), the stereotype of teenage pregnancy as a deliberate device to secure housing remains strong both in the media and the general public (Allen, 1998). However, our research demonstrates that not only is the link between independent living and the transition to adulthood a complex one, but many of the young women interviewed for this research had not intended to become pregnant and in most cases were shocked at the situation they faced.

2 The research and its context

In June 1999 the government published its report on *Teenage Pregnancy*, setting forward its agenda for the reduction of the current high rate of conceptions. The impetus for the report lay with the UK's position as the country in Western Europe with the highest rate of teenage births, a consequence of other countries successfully reducing their rates over the previous two decades. While it might also be assumed that high rates would be found in Catholic countries, France has managed to reduce its teenage pregnancy rates considerably through concerted action that supports, among other initiatives, emergency contraception in schools, the availability of both surgical and medical abortion, and extensive skills-based sex education in schools.

For the first time in a government report, the circumstances surrounding teenage pregnancy were laid out clearly. It noted that in 1997, in England:

- almost 90,000 teenagers became pregnant

- roughly three-fifths went on to give birth, 56,000 in total

- almost 7,700 conceptions were to under 16s (about 70 per cent to 15 year olds), resulting in 3,700 births

- 2,200 conceptions were to girls aged 14 or under

- around 50 per cent of conceptions to under 16s ended in abortion (Office of National Statistics, 1998).

The Report sought explanations for this continued high rate within existing research, identifying key risk factors such as poverty or low educational achievement which singly or multiply could lead to a greater risk of becoming a teenage parent. It was also noted that certain areas displayed a geographical concentration of teenage pregnancy and these same areas were often classified as the most deprived.

Figure 1 Teenage conceptions – outcome by age at conception, England 1997

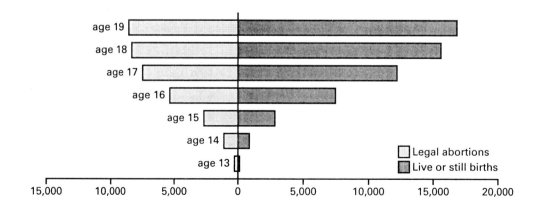

The local context

According to the figures used in the *Teenage Pregnancy* report, the area in which this research was conducted, Doncaster, is within the top 10 per cent of local authorities for teenage pregnancies and the top 44 most deprived out of 300. Social deprivation can be evidenced by (amongst others) factors related to employment, household income, educational level and morbidity and mortality rates.

Doncaster has a higher proportion of its population in manual social classes than England and Wales generally. Although classified by the Office of National Statistics as a 'mining and industrial area (coal fields)', there are few people now working in the coal industry and Doncaster is an area of high unemployment and economic deprivation. Educational achievement is poor in Doncaster, with only 34 per cent achieving five GCSEs or NVQ equivalent compared with 45 per cent for England as a whole.

The population is around 292,000 (ONS 1997 mid-year estimate), with an age structure that differs slightly from that of England and Wales: Doncaster has more children and less elderly people. Doncaster has a fairly small ethnic minority population – around 4 per cent.

The population of Doncaster is spread across the district in small towns and villages that were built around the local coalmine. Where mines have closed these towns and villages have few sources of employment for young people.

The health experience of the people of Doncaster is generally worse than in the country as a whole with an increased risk of dying before the age of 75 compared to the average English person. This is linked to deprivation.

Doncaster health services

There are 155 general practitioners (GPs) in 53 practices arranged in three primary care groups. Doncaster has difficulty attracting GPs and is relatively underprovided compared with the England average. All Doncaster GPs provide contraceptive services and at least one practice provides a nurse-led young people's contraceptive advice service.

Secondary care services are mainly provided by the Doncaster Royal and Montagu Hospitals NHS Trust, comprising a large district general hospital and a second, much smaller acute hospital. Gynaecology services and maternity services are provided within the Women's Hospital at the Doncaster Royal Infirmary. First trimester terminations are delivered under NHS contract by the local British Pregnancy Advisory Service (BPAS) clinic which is situated in the centre of Doncaster. In addition, some Doncaster residents are treated at Sheffield, Barnsley or Rotherham hospitals.

Doncaster and South Humber Health Care NHS Trust (DSHHCT) provides family planning services and there are clinics daily, except Sunday, at Chequer Road Clinic in the town centre. There are also young people's clinics including the Saturday morning 'Choices' clinic in the town centre and the 'Always' clinic at Stainforth.

Doncaster Health Authority funds 'Jigsaw', a service aimed at 15 to 25 year olds giving free confidential advice, information and counselling on any issues affecting young people's health and well-being.

Sexual health

The pattern of sexual health in Doncaster can be summarised by the following statistical data.

Figure 2 Map of Doncaster

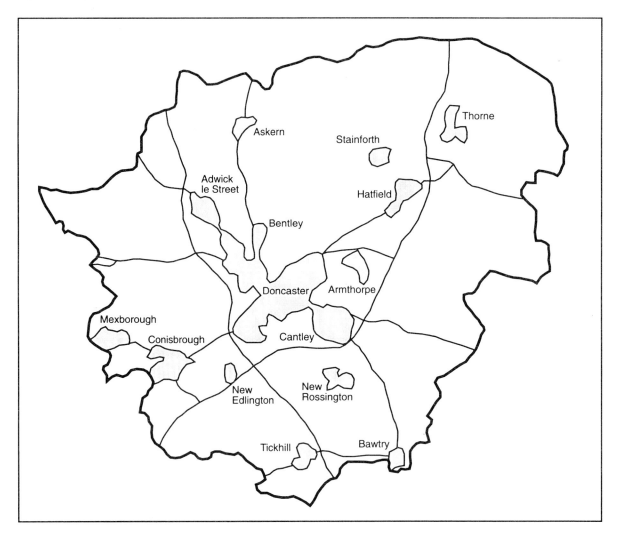

- There were 3,538 live births to Doncaster women in 1998: 23 to girls under 16 and 46 to 16 year olds.

- The general fertility rate is higher than the national rate.

- In 1997 there were 790 terminations of pregnancy, of which 28 were to girls under 16.

- On average 44 per cent of Doncaster women will have an abortion during their reproductive lifetime.

- Doncaster Health Authority District had the seventh highest rate of teenage pregnancy in the country at 13.5 per 1,000 girls aged 13 to 15 in 1995–97 (the most recent period for which figures are available).

This study, therefore, looked at the choices open to, and the decisions made by young pregnant women, in an area that is suffering from economic deprivation and where there is an exceptionally high rate of teenage pregnancy. By examining in depth the experiences of those living in one area, the aim was to look at all the factors that might influence decision making, including the response of the community itself.

3 The research design

As was noted in Chapter 2, research into teenage pregnancy has traditionally followed one of two routes: it has either concentrated on teenage conceptions as evidenced by teenage motherhood, and specifically how these can be avoided (Social Exclusion Unit, 1999), or it has looked at the experiences of young women and their children and possible reasons for subsequent disadvantage (Furstenberg, 1987; Phoenix, 1991). These two sets of literature are often conflated, with the result that issues surrounding teenage pregnancy are condensed into concerns about contraception and how to encourage responsible use in order to reduce high rates of conception and pregnancy. In Britain this objective is yet to be achieved and teenage conception rates have remained high, with a significant percentage resulting in live births to teenage mothers.

One consequence of this conflating of the issues is that there is an assumption that teenage conceptions almost automatically lead to birth. Abortion is rarely mentioned as an option in discussions about teenage pregnancy by those researching it, by policy-makers or by those young people who may need access to it.

There is clearly an important gap in our understanding of the ways in which young women decide to continue with or terminate their pregnancy. The research reported here was designed to explore the factors shaping these choices, and so help fill this gap. While there are many contingencies that influence these decisions, our data suggest important socio-cultural factors in the Doncaster area which may make it likely that teenage conception will result in births. As such, the research has an important contribution to make to policy interventions in this area (see Chapter 9).

Methodology

To examine the decision-making process and the choices open to young women faced with an unintended pregnancy, we undertook the following.

- In order to examine the decisions open to young women in this community, ten focus groups were undertaken with mostly *non-pregnant* young women between the ages of 13 and 26. These sought to ascertain their views on teenage pregnancies, young motherhood and abortion, the likely influences on any decision made and what outcomes they thought likely.

- During the second stage, 41 individual interviews were carried out with young women *who had been or were pregnant* aged 18 or under. Of these, 11 had chosen not to continue with their pregnancies. In these interviews we asked young women about the perceived influence of parents and boyfriends, especially with regard to how each group might help confirm or deny young women's decisions about teenage pregnancy as part of the transition to adulthood.

- The third stage focused attention on young men and a sample of parents to determine their attitudes towards teenage pregnancy. In order to investigate the perceived influence of young men in the decision-making process, seven focus groups were carried out with young men between the ages of 14 and 20 who, with one exception, *were not fathers* to find out their views on teenage pregnancy, young motherhood and abortion.

- Finally, 13 individual interviews were conducted with parents of teenagers *who were not pregnant* with whom issues surrounding teenage pregnancy, young motherhood and abortion were explored to ascertain what information young women gain from their families in making a decision about a pregnancy.

In all the interviews, with the exception of those with the pregnant teenagers, questions were also asked about the experience and merits of sex education.

Sample population: access and profile

Stage 1: focus groups

The focus groups for the first stage of the project were derived from various sources, principally youth clubs, and education and training establishments (see Table 1). Youth clubs were identified in areas of Doncaster which were socially disadvantaged, whilst those in education and training were from more diverse backgrounds. This purposive sampling, reflected in the composition of the groups,

helped to ensure that respondents' views were likely to be more typical of young women in Doncaster and other areas with similar levels of deprivation.

The focus group sessions (group size 4 to 9) with non-pregnant young women were analysed not only for the views expressed about teenage pregnancies but also for the negotiation and consolidation of these views within peer groups.

The main areas covered in the focus group sessions with the young women were:

- their knowledge and experience of teenage pregnancy in the communities

- their views on abortion and teenage motherhood

- sources of information and advice on contraception and pregnancy

- their views and experience of sex education

- their understanding of the possible influences and pressures on the decision to continue with a pregnancy or not.

Table 1 Sources for focus groups

Type of group	Age range	No. of participants
Sixth form (SF1)	16–17	6
Sixth form (SF2)	17–18	6
Vocational training (VT)	17–23	7
Pre-vocational training (PVT)	17–18	6
HE group (HE)	18–22	9
Youth club (YC1)	13–16	6
Youth club (YC2)	13–15	9
Young people's clinic (YC3)	14–15	4
Youth club (YC4)	13–14	6
Women's group (WG)	18–26	6

Stage 2: the interviews

The original proposal was to interview 40 young women aged 18 and under who had made the decision to continue with a pregnancy or not. It was intended that half of the sample would be young women who had chosen not to continue with their pregnancies. This distribution was difficult to secure because of problems in identifying and accessing young women who chose to have an abortion. Although those continuing with their pregnancies were equally unlikely to come forward unprompted, approaches made through agencies such as education, social services and midwives proved productive for this group. For those choosing abortion, approaches were made directly in the local abortion clinic. However, because of issues of consent these young women were aged 16 or over.

Both these access routes were somewhat unsatisfactory inasmuch as they relied on other agencies, rather than a direct approach from the researchers to the young women themselves. Given the potential sensitivity of interviewing young women who had had abortions, the research team ensured that consent was sought both a week before and immediately before interview, and that the young woman was aware that she could withdraw at any time. There were also concerns about breaches of confidentiality as most women tended to be accompanied at the clinic and wished to bring their companion into the interview. However we found that in all cases the accompanying person echoed and gave substance to the views expressed by the young woman in the interview.

It should also be noted that for the sample of teenage mothers, whilst all were or would be under 18 at birth, the sample contained a range of ages and experiences of motherhood, including some who had more than one child, some who had recently given birth and others who were pregnant. For example, of the 41 interviewed:

- seven were aged over 18 at interview

- three had had more than one child at interview

- six were pregnant at interview with their first child, average age 15

- 26 had been teenage mothers, two of which had had more than one child at interview

- 11 had had a termination of pregnancy whilst a teenager

- three had had a pregnancy followed by a termination

- the average age at first pregnancy was just under 16.

Such a range of experience presented us with the opportunity to see not only what influences decisions at the time, but also what the young women might think of their reasons retrospectively, and how any future decisions might differ in the light of experience. For example, we found that once a child was born, abortion was more likely to be considered for subsequent pregnancies.

The main areas covered in the individual interviews with the pregnant young women were:

- their living and working circumstances at conception

- their use of contraception and reasons for any non-use

- influences on the decision to continue with the pregnancy or have an abortion

- their response to any future pregnancy

- any advice to others facing a similar choice.

Our experience here parallels that of previous studies that have found teenage mothers and abortion patients difficult groups to access. Overall however, after careful follow-up, the methods adopted here did result in a substantial, forthcoming and valuable sample.

Stage 3: focus groups with young men and interviews with parents

The focus group sessions (group size 4 to 9) with young men who were not fathers were undertaken with volunteers from Doncaster's New Deal programme and youth clubs. Again these access routes were targeted at young men who were likely to be less socially advantaged and among whom friends and peers would be likely to have experienced teenage pregnancy. In total:

- five groups were carried out with young men aged 16 to 20 on New Deal

- two groups were carried out with young men aged 14 to 16 in areas of Doncaster that were identified as having social and economic problems.

The main areas covered with the young men in the focus group sessions were:

- their use of contraception and expectations of conception

- their experience of sex education and its value to them

- their view on and experience of teenage motherhood and abortion

- the role of fathers in deciding to continue with a pregnancy or not

- the long-term role of fathers and their expectations of their own future.

The interviews with parents were undertaken to determine:

- their views on and participation in sex education

- their views and concerns on teenage pregnancy and abortion

- their preferred options should a pregnancy arise

- their potential role in helping their son or daughter to decide whether to continue with a pregnancy or not

- the type of support they would make available

- their expectations for their son or daughter.

Parents were identified through various routes, including personal and professional contacts in order to achieve a wide spectrum of social circumstances and attitudes.

Comment on focus groups

The data produced by the focus group method appeared to demonstrate a clear watershed in peer interaction and discussion in relation to both age and gender (Fritz and Kitzinger, 1998). Under the age of 16 (for young women) and 17 (for young men) peer pressure and peer influence in exploring issues related to teenage pregnancy and sexuality was very much more in evidence in group interactions. For these younger age groups, individuals seemed to have less formed opinions and to be less willing to express or defend them than the older groups. Group gender formation appeared also to play an important role in how opinions were expressed, with the younger men sometimes participating in displays of bravado, boasting and machismo, which clearly shaped individual disclosures in a group setting.

Although focus groups are artificial groups with an outsider present, they may give us some flavour of the peer pressures that act to police discussion of such sensitive issues, particularly for the youngest. Whilst any individual may think differently and have different experiences from his/her peers, the nature of group interaction suggests these differences may never come to be heard in a group. For young men, this effectively bounds discussion within what Connell has called the terms of hegemonic masculinity, which forbids the expression of emotions, experiences or desires that may be in any way seen as soft or feminine (Prendergast and Forrest, 1997). The opposite might be true for young women who may find it difficult to express needs or desires that might conflict with idealised notions of femininity, particularly the desire to become a mother. Clearly these factors are key in mediating the power of peer groups in thinking about pregnancy. It may also be that with age and experience, the more individuated and realistic their thinking, with less significance placed upon the power of peers.

Despite obvious limitations, the broader methodological value of the focus group technique is its capacity to illuminate shared cultures among the peer members who make it up, and tendencies towards views likely to be shared by the wider community. They also, in contrast to individual interviews, provide an opportunity to test beliefs among the respondents and to stimulate debate that reveals a variety of opinions on the topics under review. Cross-analysis of the various focus groups enabled the research to identify common elements found in the wider culture of the young men – for example, in relation to views about responsibility for contraception – as well as perspectives on relationships with partners.

Each of the research methods used presented a challenge for the research team. In respect of the sample, whilst ideally all the respondents would have come forward without prompting and without the support of intervening agencies, such a response was not forthcoming and other ways of accessing young people had to be found. Whilst these routes were not always ideal, they did ultimately prove successful. Once at the interview or in the focus group the young people were generally interested in the research and willing to give their time and views.

4 Setting the parameters for the decision

There is evidence that the under 16s are most at risk of not using contraception, particularly at first intercourse (Fleissig, 1991; Metson, 1991). Even when younger women do use potentially reliable methods they experience a failure rate higher than women aged 25 or over. This problematic use has been associated with a lack of education or information and infrequent (or non-) use of contraceptives by young people, based on beliefs about the pros and cons of some forms of contraception and difficulties with access. These two aspects of unplanned conception have been highlighted recently by the government's report on teenage pregnancy, together with an action plan including new guidelines for sex education and projects designed at changing young people's contraceptive use.

Sex education

The young people in this study confirmed this evidence. They felt that they lacked information and expressed doubts as to the value of formal sex education as taught at school. It was often seen as irrelevant with too much emphasis on biology and not enough on feelings and emotions. Teaching staff were perceived to be embarrassed and the content of the lessons was regarded as inappropriate, boring and too late. There was doubt expressed by both the young men and young women in the focus groups as to the value of sex education in informing or helping them in the decision when to have sex or in preventing pregnancies under 16.

Q *So do you think that the sex education that you had at school helped you decide when to have sex?*

X *No.*

W *There's a difference isn't there between if you love somebody or if it is just like a washing machine. Didn't learn about that at school though did you?*

Q *No. So do you think sex education helped you decide when to have sex?*

W *No ... Half of them had already done it anyway.*

Q *Did it help you make any decisions?*

W *No. (New Deal 1)*

Rather, other factors, including peer group pressure and the pressure from a boyfriend could prove crucial.

Q *But you can't stop the boy?*

B *No it's like they pressurise you.*

C *They persuade you don't they?*

B *If you really like him you're going to do it aren't you?*

C *Otherwise they're going to split up with you. And you don't want them to because you really like them or something like that. (YC2)*

Doubt as to the worth of formal sex education in school was also expressed by parents who thought that young people gathered most of their knowledge about sex from their peers, the television – such as *The Jerry Springer Show* – and, (for young women) from magazines. Parents were conscious of their lack of credibility and influence.

I think it's from their mates. Er, parents could be seen as nagging and 'Oh, shut up', you know, 'I'm ...' – they tend to know it all, they're more likely to take notice of their mates than they are of their parents. (Pam)

I think more of the TV as it is not dictating to them saying you must do this or that or the other, but just steer them in a certain way, like these will say 'Mother stop giving me a lecture', and then you have lost it then. (Brenda)

Dismissal of school-based sex education did not mean however that all parents were proactive in their own approach to sex education with their children. Whilst some had used books or approached the subject directly, others took a more laid back approach, especially the parents of sons.

With Jeremy I must admit I didn't so much ... Obviously I said you know the facts of life, but I told him about condoms when he was about twelve, and about wet dreams, ... But with Mary I went through the Usborne book, Growing up, don't know if you've ever seen it, it's a really good book, and we went through it, from cover to cover, covering every topic that come through, and I said, 'Do you understand all this?'. (Marion)

No, no, I've always waited for them to ask me, because I don't think you should impose on them – it's like respecting that they will come to you when they know they're ready. (Meryl)

Lack of willingness to engage in discussion about sex with either peers or parents was also expressed by the young men's focus groups, where they recounted an absence of sources of information from both parents and school. The prospect of discussing sex with parents was embarrassing for both parties.

K They should really, they should both teach you, it's just funny – it's when your parents –

I'd rather be sat down at school in a class with me mates talking about it than standing there on your own with your mum and dad chatting in front of you.

T You just don't want to talk about it with your mum and dad. Not the sort of thing you like to talk about, is it? (Youth club 1)

Their conversations about sex were usually restricted to their mates or 'having a joke' with their fathers rather than any serious discussion.

Q So you can talk about sex with your parents?

T I can't – I'm embarrassed.

R I'm not, you know what me dad's like!

Q Embarrassed to what?

T Talk about sex.

S Slept at his house, right, and his dad's giving me full lecture on it – telling me what he's done, telling me all positions! 'Stand 'em on their head and it's easy to drop in ...' he says 'Stand 'em on their head and you don't have to do no work'. (Youth club 2)

Making light of a potentially embarrassing subject, however, was also seen as an effective way to get a message across by one of the parents.

I have talked about them messing around and that ... 'There's nothing to be embarrassed about', I said, 'but I'd like to know, let me know, I can help you', I said, 'if you want, I could ... get up the clinic, or I can come to the doctor's with you, you want to do it on your own, sort it out!' ... I was saying, 'Look, you can get all you can want, lovely colours, different tastes, different textures, you get strawberry ones, banana, there's all sorts', I

said, 'it doesn't have to be boring. Oh, hang on,
I've just got to put my condom on' I said, you can
have fun. (William)

Use of contraception

Lack of formal information sources did not
however mean that young people were unaware
of contraception or that in most cases they did
not use it.

Young people, however, saw disadvantages
to the contraceptives available. Condoms were
difficult to access and to use, whilst some young
women stated that they had got pregnant whilst
on the Pill, citing the use of antibiotics as
contributing to its failure. No young women in
the sample had used or considered the morning
after pill.

The non-users of contraception who became
pregnant should not be regarded as a group
who sought pregnancy. They were long-term
none or intermittent users due to factors
external to the sexual relationship. These
included problems with gaining contraception
from health professionals, a belief in their own
or their partners' infertility often due to drug

**Table 2 Contraceptives used by 41 young women
at time of conception**

Method	Number
None	17
Condoms	7
The Pill	7
The Pill + condom	1
Injection	1
Other *	6
Info missing	2
Total	**41**

* Includes intermittent use/forgot Pill.

use, or parental intervention in contraception.

Thus the majority of young women in the
sample appeared to be aware of contraception,
and in some, but not all cases, were taking some
precautions to prevent pregnancy. Young
women gave a variety of reasons for non-use of
contraception, including practical reasons of
access and beliefs that, as they had not already
become pregnancy, their luck would hold in the
future.

R   I thought I'd never get pregnant I thought, I
     haven't got pregnant so far so why should I
     now. (Rebecca)

These interviews reflected commonly held
views in the focus groups, where a tendency not
to use contraception was felt to be a normal part
of young relationships.

Q   So people don't know about contraceptives?

L   They are aware but just can't be bothered.

N   I think younger ones aren't aware that you can
     get it.

A   Think it can't happen to them. (VT)

Q   Why would a girl of 16 get pregnant?

F   Because they don't use contraception
     enough.

X   Because the boys force them into it.

S   They are not aware of how easy it is to get
     pregnant and how hard it is to look after a
     baby. (YC4)

For many of the young women in the sample
their pregnancy came as a shock. They had not
planned it or even considered the possibility
previously and some had believed it impossible.

Once the pregnancy was confirmed all were forced to consider their immediate and long-term options in a short space of time.

Gender relations

Some of the problems with using condoms were expanded upon in the focus groups with young men. While declaring that responsibility for contraception should be shared by the couple, the groups nevertheless went on to argue that it is the young women's responsibility to be on the Pill if they want to avoid pregnancy. Clearly in their view it is women who are at risk and therefore it is their responsibility.

> *It's her responsibility and you, you want sex, you ask, you say – you know what I mean, and if she says she's on Pill that's it! – she gets it, doesn't she. If she's not, that's her problem, isn't it?* (Youth club 2)

Young men also described practical difficulties with accessing condoms for their own protection. Whilst all knew where condoms could be obtained, access points were seen as problematic. Buying from shops made condoms too expensive, whilst going to a family planning clinic was thought to be embarrassing. Once a young woman was on the Pill these potential barriers to contraception were removed or rather became her responsibility, regardless of how effectively she was taking it.

> B *My girlfriend just takes it any time during day.*
>
> N *Well, that's wrong then.*
>
> C *That's wrong. You're going to be a dad soon.*
>
> B *There's been times, right, where she hasn't taken it for a couple of days and she's just took like, say she hasn't took it for two days*

> *and she's just took, like, three.*
>
> N *Congratulations!*
>
> B *We've been alright! It's either me firing blanks or ...* (New Deal 2)

In many cases not only were young men willing to hand over total responsibility for contraception and the safety of its day to day use to young women, but at the same time they then believed themselves to be protected. If it was the young women's responsibility, young men themselves were less culpable and less responsible in the event of an unwanted pregnancy.

This very limited notion of risk in relation to teenage fatherhood, almost its denial, together with the different kinds of risks taken by young women, suggests that there is still much work to be done in understanding young people's assessment of risk in early sexual relationships, the prevention of pregnancy and the consequences of an early pregnancy for the young woman involved. Indeed, in the context of these gender relations around the usage of contraceptives it is surprising that many more young women do not become pregnant.

Teenage motherhood in the family

In their interviews parents described how (in contrast to sex education) teenage pregnancy was often discussed in the family due to its visibility among peer groups and the community.

> *And there's a young girl who lives across road from us, she had a baby just recently, at 15, so she was actually 14 when she got pregnant, and, and my daughter was just like 'Well, I'm going to*

be a virgin when I get married!' She was just sort
of disgusted by the thought of being a mum.
(Trisha)

This had lead to discussions about how parents would react if their own daughter (or son) announced that they were having a baby.

If she does come home at 16 she knows I won't
throw her out but she knows I won't be a full
time babysitter for her ... She can stop under my
roof and I will feed and clothe them ... Those are
the rules if she stops under my roof, I won't kick
her out anyway, that's when they get into a lot
more trouble, if you kick them out. (Brenda)

The young women in the focus groups who were not pregnant were also aware of the support they could expect from their own parents if they did become pregnant. This support was seen as part of a natural extension of the everyday reliance on their parents they experienced as children.

If you're like younger they'll say, 'Oh you don't
know what you're doing, you're not mature
enough to look after it, we'll help you'. But if
you're like 16 they might just not help you and tell
you to look after it on your own, and they might
kick you out, then you've got nowhere to live.
(YC2)

Coupled with this advance knowledge of support within their own families, young women were also aware of the support experienced by their family and friends who had also been pregnant. The unconditional support of parents was also found among the parents of non-pregnant teenage daughters who stated that support would be offered regardless of any initial shock or disappointment at a

pregnancy. For young women, knowledge of this support could be instrumental in the decision made.

Interestingly, the young men too discussed this issue, often with a sense that they were missing out on parental attention and care compared to young women. In contrast, they noted that fathers could boast about and encourage sons' sexual exploits, welcoming them into the world of adult men. This is similar to the greater parental attention paid to and control over girls' sexuality noted in the WRAP study. In the focus groups the young men also expressed a double standard in regard to women's sexuality, sharing a view, for example, that although their own sexual exploits were a laugh, and the girl who took the risk a fool, they would be outraged and beat up any boy that got their sister pregnant.

It's just a thing you think, 'my little sister' isn't it,
and if anyone hurt your sister you'd, now you
know how your dad did – like if my daughter got
pregnant I'd kill him. For some reason it's just,
first thing that comes into your head, 'What's he
done to my daughter?' same with me sister.
(New Deal 3)

Abortion in the family

In contrast to teenage motherhood, abortion was not generally discussed in families and most parents were not aware of anyone who had had an abortion. Support thought to be required from parents under these conditions was assumed to be more emotional than practical, it often included 'being there' for the daughter and attending the clinic if necessary, helping her through a potentially traumatic experience.

I'd just be here for her, em, any questions that she ... if I thought I could help her, answer questions ... em, just try and make her understand that the decision she'd made was the right one, basically, she'd decided to terminate it, and just be here for her, if she felt she needed us. (Brenda)

Although most of the parents stated that they would offer support to their daughters or sons if an abortion was their decision, the young women choosing this option did not feel that such support was available, perhaps because it was something that wasn't discussed. Most of the young women choosing abortion had told only a small group of close family and friends, sometimes not even telling their parents or boyfriends and feeling forced to devise elaborate cover-up stories.

I told my parents, because I was due to start college on the day I had to go to hospital, I told them I was staying a night at friends the previous night because I knew I could come out. I had to stay in overnight and knew I could come out the next day. So that was the cover-up story, I was at a friend's, had to go to college the next day and then I'd come home as though I'd been home from college. (Sam)

But where they did have someone to talk to this could prove decisive in their thinking.

I'd been stopping at me boyfriend's house and a girl called Jacky who I know were there, and she'd already got a little girl, and she helped me, talked through it, and she's had an abortion as well after she'd had her little girl she's got, so ... I'd been talking to her ... (Annabelle)

Yeah, 'cos I went to see a woman who lives

across road from me stepmum, and she were telling me she were pregnant when she were 15 and she had an abortion, she said that it hurt her, but it were for best reasons ... (Lauren)

Teenage pregnancy in the wider community

Whilst all the young people stated that the knowledge and information they had derived from sex education would not help them cope with an unexpected pregnancy, they often drew upon and quoted a range of experiences of teenage pregnancy from within their communities.

Both young women and young men stated that there were areas of Doncaster where teenage pregnancy was seen as being particularly high. These areas were those in which economic decline had been brought about by the decline in mining industries.

It depends what area they're living in, because if it is somewhere, next mining village, they've not got things to want to give it [the pregnancy] up. (SF2)

It was felt that in these areas early pregnancy, at 15 or 16 was understandable and justifiable, but under this age it was less acceptable. In other areas teenage pregnancy was not felt to be so understandable, although it remained a visible part of community life. Once a pregnancy was confirmed news of it spread fast and it was assumed that a decision had been made to continue.

Q So has she decided to have it?

M Yes, well yes, because it has gone round everyone now anyway, so I would say that

she has ... because she wouldn't tell
everyone if she wouldn't, would she? (Lara)

Abortion in the wider community

This apparent social acceptance of pregnancy was in stark contrast to the apparent invisibility and closure around the experience of abortion in the wider community. Abortion was not mentioned in relation to school sex education, generally avoided by parents and not discussed even by young women who had had one.

Socially then, abortion stands in complete contrast to the option of teenage motherhood. Young women therefore faced choosing a known, and relatively common social outcome, teenage motherhood, or an invisible, unknown one, abortion.

Q *Do you think you've not known anyone who's had an abortion because people don't talk about abortions or, because people haven't had them?*

L *Your friends talk about pregnancy and abortion but you always talk if you were pregnant and what you'd do and then like you think about other things, but I've never known anyone to be pregnant and have an abortion. I've known people to be pregnant and have a miscarriage.* (YC3)

For the young women in the focus groups abortion was seen as an unsatisfactory end to a pregnancy.

I don't know what people feel like when they get an abortion, I've never had one, and never want to have one. But I think in a way, it's a bad way to get rid of a child. Because you'll have the chance of life, your mum could have just said no. They

gave you the chance of life, and you've had a chance to have a life so you should give that baby one chance. (YC2)

Abortion was also associated with being bullied or hounded out of school.

Q *What would happen if everyone knew at school that somebody had had an abortion?*

T *You wouldn't be able to go to school.*

G *You'd get called. You'd probably get hit an' all, wouldn't you.* (YC4)

Where abortion was chosen if knowledge of it became public, these anticipated negative reactions were experienced.

You can't really say people were helpful; there were people who annoyed you! ... Who kept saying 'Oh, no, you want to keep it!', and 'Oh, you can't do that!' and 'Doesn't it make you feel guilty?'; you just want to slap 'em really ... Wish they'd shut up! (Stacey)

I told this woman I knew who I worked with and she turned round and called me a murderer. (Lucy)

These remarks suggest that even after the decision to have an abortion is made the acceptance of this by others in the community may be difficult, leading to abortion being kept a secret and thereby remaining hidden despite the numbers who do opt for this choice.

Comments

These findings suggest that faced with an unplanned pregnancy the decisions that a young woman makes are likely to be influenced by factors outside of the immediate situation, even if she claims the decision for herself. As it stands the balance of these factors would appear to encourage both conception and once conceived, the pursuit of the pregnancy. Control over sexual encounters or pregnancy prevention through current methods of formal sex education or the use of contraception, seem to have little impact on the decision making between sexual partners. At the same time, factors related to the informal, cultural framing of sexuality and pregnancy by the community and conventional gender relations are likely to bring about both initial conception and the subsequent sustaining of the pregnancy. We have already noted in Chapter 2 that only half of pregnancies to those under 16 end in childbirth, so there are clearly other factors at work within the family, household, peer group and more widely that shape the eventual decision to go to term. Before we can begin to tie these down, we need to explore in more detail the ways in which this decision making as a process takes place.

5 Making the decision

Regardless of the pregnancy outcome almost all of the young women interviewed were shocked at finding themselves pregnant and had not planned to be pregnant. For some the actual discovery of the pregnancy itself had been a difficult period, taking place in some instances over many months as they went through a series of pregnancy tests from a variety of agencies and sought to understand the changes taking place in their bodies.

> It turned out that I went for one pregnancy test, I was putting weight on and ... I remember Brian saying, 'You must be pregnant you are really fat' and I was devastated. Anyway I went for one test, it's a free one in town. Is it Life? So I went there and have a free pregnancy test, and they told me there and then that I weren't pregnant. So I said right but I hadn't had any periods, and I was putting weight on and I was thinking am I going through menopause or what? I'm thinking what's wrong with me, so I brushed it off, tried to forget about it but obviously you can't really. I was off booze as well, I couldn't drink, it's not like me something like that ... so I had another one and it said it was negative again, so I'm thinking I can't be pregnant but what's wrong with me. (Fiona)

Once a pregnancy was confirmed the young women were faced with making a decision about continuing the pregnancy, often very quickly, with or without the support of others. Perhaps not surprisingly in light of the short time available, influences on this decision were often derived from their own existing views and the known experiences of those surrounding them, particularly with respect to abortion and teenage motherhood.

Views on abortion and motherhood

Within those interviewed, often the decision to continue with the pregnancy was made very quickly based upon their views, which were often anti-abortion, especially those expressed by young women who had yet to give birth. These views were linked to the idea of babies as sources of love and the notion that the teenage mother should take responsibility rather than making an 'innocent' baby suffer.

> So if you're going to make a child I know in some cases you can't keep the child in certain circumstances but I never used protection, it's not the baby's fault, so I've got to go through with it, so it's wrong to take a baby away. (Judy)

> The biggest dream a girl could have is getting pregnant and having a baby, you know that when you are old you've got somebody there for you. (Jane)

Opinions on abortion and motherhood often changed after the birth of the child and particularly as it reached toddlerhood.

> It was just I could see this baby, it's a right sunny day, I'm going to be walking down the street and I've got this baby and it's asleep, and all my mates are going to come up and be right envious, but it don't work out like that, usually the babies are crying. You have like daydreams and things like when you are pregnant, like we'd never experienced stuff like this before. You make stuff up in your head and you think it's true, like you see babies on telly and they are asleep all the time. (Debbie)

This experience of the demands of motherhood led a significant number of the women to state that if they were to fall pregnant again whilst their baby was still young they would have an abortion regardless of their previous views on this. So when asked if she would make the same decision again this young woman replied:

No, I don't think so. I'm finding it hard to cope with him. (Cindy)

Such a finding suggests that first motherhood is a watershed in terms of thinking about abortion. Once achieved and the reality of dealing with a baby experienced, other factors might be permitted to influence decisions about whether or not to continue a pregnancy. These might include the welfare of their existing child and their own ability to cope with any more children.

This was borne out by the interviews with those young women who did choose abortion, two of whom already had young children and were shocked at finding themselves pregnant again within a short space of time. Indeed these two felt forced to have an abortion.

I have had an abortion since, about three week ago and that were best decision for me because I, well I could cope with another baby but I can't financially support it. (Stacey)

'Cos I've never ever really thought of me doing something like this, not at all ... not at all. But I've got myself into the situation where I really needed to really help myself cope with what I've already got. (Diane)

This young woman was not happy about the decision she was making but as she already had a young son she felt that this was the best option. The child she already had took precedence over the new pregnancy and

overcame her previous scruples.

This dislike of abortion and fear of medical intervention was instrumental in some decisions to continue with the pregnancy.

It's not that I wanted to have a baby I didn't want to have an abortion. If there was a tablet that I could have taken to get rid, I would have done it, but I wasn't having an abortion. (Janice)

Yeah, but I think ... a lot of the reason why I didn't have an abortion was probably 'cos I was scared ... you get all these, you imagine all this gory stuff about when you have an abortion, 'cos people don't inform you, but having had an abortion, now, it's nowt ... honest, it's just ... I went in with in mind like, I'm having an em, operation, and that's all it is, they knock you out and wake you up. (Stacey)

Once the experience of abortion is known it fails to live up to the traumatic experience anticipated.

Even for the young women who did choose abortion there was an initial reluctance to consider this option. In many cases circumstances were blamed such as their family, relationship, their plans for the future or the conditions in which conception occurred.

No, I just went out one night and got drunk and it was over and done with before I knew what I was doing. (Sandra)

However, those in our sample who had decided to continue with their pregnancies had also had similar considerations to think about, but had made a different decision, due to their unwillingness to consider abortion.

I didn't have a boyfriend, I wasn't in a relationship or anything it was not a party, something that happened after getting drunk, something that I regretted, and then it was chucked in my face again. (Debbie)

Likewise, the young women who made different decisions about whether to continue with their pregnancies or not, had similar educational backgrounds and hopes for the future. However, the sample who chose abortion tended to be older – due to issues of parental consent – and more of them had left school.

This might suggest that school is relatively easier to drop out of than working, or 'having a life', post-school, particularly if attendance is sporadic or non-existent.

I needed to mature a little bit, basically because I was stupid, but now I'm back at school I'm going for my qualifications and I know that I can pass them because I'm not getting put down anymore. Before I was pregnant I was never at school for a year and a half. Now I am going to do all I can. (Jane)

Moreover, for some young women having a baby was an impetus to sort their lives out and to focus on the future, as shown by Moira who had been a truant prior to her first pregnancy at 14.

I'm at college at the moment actually and I'm doing sociology and I'm doing a project on teenage pregnancy, and the reasons for the increase in teenage pregnancy. And I'm hoping next year to get them into the crèche at college and do a full time course or something. I can't stay at home. It annoys me sitting at home doing nothing all day. I'd like to become a primary school teacher I think eventually. (Moira)

Rather than an end to ambitions or aspirations in some cases the birth of a child was regarded as a positive life experience in respect to education, particularly for the young women – like those above – who went to a dedicated centre for young parents.

It is also notable that a significant number of young women were already working when they discovered their pregnancy and chose to have an abortion. This might suggest that once school has been left behind young women might be more inclined to consider abortion; however, this is disputed by the number of young mothers who were working at the time of their pregnancy and who had, or intended to return to work or college later. Rather, what was crucial to the decision of these young women was their views on abortion and motherhood and the support of those views by those closest

Table 3 Outcome of pregnancy in different situations

Situation	Birth	Abortion
School	14	1
Truant	6	1
Unemployed/stay at home mothers*	5	4
College	2	2
Working	7	3

*Two mothers chose to have a subsequent abortion, and two chose to continue with subsequent pregnancies. One young woman who had had an abortion, continued with a later pregnancy

to them. Where such support was absent, this caused considerable resentment.

> *He was older than I was even though it was five years, he was 21 nearly 22, there was five years there. Five years on a bloke to a girl of that age is a lot, he should have been mature, he should have said 'Come on this isn't right for you'.* (Belinda)

In the focus groups with the young men, although abortion was in general condemned, different views about it were expressed depending on the relationship in which conception took place. On the one hand, in a long-term relationship an abortion was regarded as unnatural and unthinkable. If necessary they claimed they would take responsibility for a child rather than 'allow' their partner to have an abortion. On the other hand, abortion might be the accepted outcome of some types of behaviour, if, for example, it was the result of a one-night stand, or if the woman was in some respects not a good mother.

> *Say you went to a nightclub, you went out, like a nightclub, you did her, she were pregnant, she's not going to know where you are or where you live so ... she's bound to have an abortion.* (New Deal 4)

Parents and other family members

Whilst most young women's parents had insisted on the decision to continue with a pregnancy being the young women's alone, the young women were aware of their parents' feelings on abortion. Other members of the family, sisters, brothers, aunts and grandmothers could also be involved and

together they could be instrumental in shaping the outcome. As Lara demonstrates in her decision to continue:

> *Mum doesn't believe in it either.* (Lara)

Parents' apparent unwillingness to influence their daughter's decision by advising her one way or the other was often backed by offers of unconditional support whatever decision she made. This in itself often acted as an important influence on the decision. The knowledge that as a teenage mother they would not be on their own and still considered as a part of their family was crucial to many young women in their decision to continue.

> *If my mum and dad said they wouldn't support me I think that would have changed my mind, because I wouldn't have been able to afford to look after her.* (Leone)

Where attempted parental influence was strong, the young woman was thrown back upon her own resources to either resist her parents and face possible ostracism from her family, or to persevere in the hope of bringing her parents round to her point of view.

> *I wanted it for me but with family falling out with me, was it best to do as they say? I'd had enough of it, you know all silent treatment and everyone and I were like I gave them an ultimatum and said, 'Alright I'll get rid of it if you can live with yourselves. You'll be left with guilt, that I've done something like this for you and then will you talk to me again?' They were like 'we don't want it to go like that' then alright with me and came round.* (Debbie)

In some cases pressure brought to bear by parents and other family members was successful, although this could lead to simmering resentment.

> My nan wanted to see me and I went to see her and she said 'Make us happy Susie' something like that, 'make us happy'. So me and Trevor had a talk on our own and he said 'If you want to keep the child keep it', so I did. (Susie)

However for most of the young women such extreme manipulation was not the norm. Rather as their parents took a step back, they felt there were few people to whom they could talk and who were willing to advise them. For some this lack of information was especially hard as it meant that the decision to continue was made in a vacuum with a lack of knowledge about abortion or any other options.

> When I went to the doctor's and told them I was pregnant she just gave me some folic acid. I just said 'I'm pregnant' and she went 'Oh right here's some folic acid'. And I were like no-one is talking to me I need to talk to someone, I was an emotional wreck. Someone might talk to me but I needed to talk to someone and it wasn't there. (Debbie)

For those who chose to have an abortion, parental involvement was also important. Not only were some mothers in attendance at the clinic but their arguments were seen in some cases to be instrumental in determining the final outcome. Although the young woman would always claim the decision herself, it was evident that the choice made was partly the result of deliberate intervention by the mother to remind her of her responsibilities.

> She didn't really say anything, she just said, 'Whatever your decision, I'm here for you, I'll stand by you', she said 'I'm not going to say anything, so I don't want you to think I'm forcing you but before you make a decision just think about, you know, like, (paying for) your horses, whatever'. (Rose)

Like those who chose to continue with their pregnancies, for those who had an abortion sometimes parental intervention was extreme and could lead to adverse outcomes.

> Well, me mum didn't find out while just before Christmas, she said 'You should have told me', and she went absolutely off her head, and she give me a choice, and like, she told me that I had to choose my family or a baby. So I did worst thing I could do, and chose family, and like, a few months after, I ended up in care – so I wish I'd never. (Sheila)

Boyfriends and their families

The boyfriends of the young women interviewed were on average 4.5 years older than the young women with the largest age difference being 16 years. Generally in our sample, the younger the woman the wider the gap in age between herself and her boyfriend. These young men could be influential on any decision made about the pregnancy.

Two of the young women who chose abortions cited their boyfriends as the reason for their abortion and blamed them for it, whilst others had discussed the situation with their boyfriends and come to the decision together.

> Q So did anyone give you any advice, did anyone say, 'You should do this' or ...?
>
> L Well, no, I wish they had done! I wish they'd said! The only person that was giving me

advice was [boyfriend] 'Get rid of it!', 'Get rid of it!' (Lisa)

It was the choice, him or the baby. (Sam)

I told him before that I thought I were, he said 'Right, well get it checked out, find out if you are' and I says 'Yeah', he says, 'right, well go round to (the) doctor's, sort it out'. So I got everything sorted out and then I went for my consultation and he came with me ...! (Stacey)

For those who continued with their pregnancy, boyfriends could also be instrumental if they held strong views on abortion and were in a relationship where those views were known.

He wouldn't talk about options that I might have had, he wouldn't even talk about it, not that I would have done, but it would have been nice to talk about the options. (Jo)

However young men were often happy to let their girlfriend take the decision alone or in association with her parents, which could in some situations contribute to a protracted period of indecision on the part of the young woman.

He was very comforting and he didn't say a lot, but then he saw me reaction, and was like 'Oh well have a termination then'. So from the start we were going to get rid of the baby, but all the way through I'm thinking it's my little baby, it were awful knowing you had a baby ... So anyway ... they booked me in and they went through everything, and the worst thing was filling out the papers. I was on the edge of tears all the time. I wanted to try and not listen and get through it, and ... he said 'I love you, and have the baby

please, don't kill our baby, I'll look after you and I'll support you and we'll get a house and all that', and then I couldn't do it. (Fiona)

Equally boyfriends' parents could have a decisive role, not only in influencing their sons but also in applying pressure for one decision rather than another.

His parents lived at the house, he told his parents, and they sat there constantly the whole three to four weeks that I sat there deciding what to do about Ben, they said if you get rid of that child you are murdering my grandchild. (Belinda)

This persuasion was not always successful and could sometimes have the opposite effect to that intended.

At first he was pleased about it and then after a month his mum were having a go at him, saying stuff to him about it, so he asked me to get rid of it. I said I wouldn't and he said 'Fair enough I'll stick by you whatever'. (Janice)

For other young women, boyfriends were seen as peripheral to both the decision to continue with the pregnancy and any continuing support, either because the relationship was not regarded as being as important as the forthcoming baby, or because parental support had already been secured.

To me, men have some say but not a lot really, they think they've got a big say in it but, they haven't really, not really ... (Diane)

Comments

These findings suggest that when a young woman has to deal with the decision whether or not to continue with an unplanned pregnancy, she is faced by a lack of information as to her choices and a reluctance on the part of those surrounding her to express an opinion. In addition young women may face uncertainty and delay in confirming their pregnancy. Together the lack of information and delay may mean that young women have little time in which to reflect upon the choices before them. In these circumstances they often fall back upon their own values and those of the community in which they live in making a decision, a community in which, as has already been noted, teenage pregnancy is highly visible and abortion invisible. When advice is offered, particularly from parents, this can be decisive, but a balance needs to be struck between advice and interference, which the young women will either reject or resent. Overall evidence suggests that sources of impartial advice are few and provision of such advice might have an effect on both the choices young women make and their ability to cope with those choices subsequently.

6 Reactions to the decision

During the decision-making process young women will weigh up the options open to them, both those presented to them by others and those that they feel are morally right for themselves. This process may include a rehearsing of different decisions and their outcomes before a final and definite route is decided upon. As described in Chapter 5, one of the groups most tested in the decision-making period are the parents of the pregnant teenager. However during this time, which is often both short and pressured, our findings suggest that both young people and parents draw upon previously established assumptions, knowledge and experiences which have evolved over possibly many years, as well as more general discussion about such issues. In this fashion, the options available to a young woman are in some ways already known.

Capture of the pregnancy by the family

Indications of how the family would respond to a teenage pregnancy were in most cases substantiated by the experiences of the young women after conception. Once a pregnancy was announced and after a period of reflection, a decision would be made and the process of what we have called 'capture' would begin. This process is signalled in the accounts of the parents, particularly mothers in their willingness to integrate the child into their existing families and was experienced with ambivalence by the young women. On the one hand this support was extremely welcome and in many cases the pregnancy may not have proceeded without it. On the other it could also be experienced as a process of enclosure and continued dependence on their family of origin.

Young women talked of their parents 'coming round' and accepting the pregnancy after a period of initial shock, often linked to the discovery that not only was their daughter having sex, but was also pregnant. This shock was often described as being particularly hard for fathers to deal with.

Well my dad is a pigeon flyer, he just went and sat in his shed because he didn't know what to do. My mum started crying but then she said 'I knew something like this were going to happen'. She were alright, she said 'I won't make you get rid of it' because my mum had to get rid of one when she were little. (Barbara)

When the pregnancy test showed up positive, my mum comforted me and my dad walked around house, was going to kill me. Then after that was alright. (Lara)

However the shock was soon dissipated when a decision was made, even if in the mind of the young woman the decision was not definitive.

Q   What about your mum? How did she react?

K   The first thing she said to me was 'Don't go near people who are smoking. Start taking folic acid'. She was trying to think of the best thing to do because I was already three months and I wasn't on a special diet or taking folic acid. So she said 'Start taking this straight away'. (Katy)

At first they said it will ruin your life, but then when I decided they were happy for me. I told them I wanted to keep it and told them that day that I wanted to keep it and they were fine. (Shelley)

Parents seemed relieved that a decision had been made and that they were now able to concentrate on developing a solution to the problem presented to them, by nursing their daughter through the pregnancy.

Capture of pregnancy was most clearly visible in those families where the young women continued to live with their parents, during the pregnancy and after the birth of the child. In some cases the boyfriend moved into the young woman's family home.

Q   So it's just you, you and your boyfriend and
    your children?

J   Yes and my mum and dad. (Judy)

But it was also visible in families where the young woman had got her own house and was outwardly independent.

I've got my own house and I live with the father,
the baby's dad. I'm still dependent on my mum.
She picks me and my son up in the morning and
takes him to Brian's mum, so that she has him
while I'm at work. So I'm still very dependent on
her. She takes me shopping and everything.
(Fiona)

In this way the children of young mothers were very quickly adopted by the extended family and integrated within it. Parents, especially, but not exclusively mothers were very important in this capture and normalisation of teenage pregnancy.

Capture of the pregnancy by the wider community

Once a decision is made it is not only the family of the teenager who become involved in the

pregnancy as the wider community and those who have a professional role become aware and start to manage it. Involved at an early stage might be those professionals with whom young women have day to day contact. For example, teachers and youth workers were found to be helpful by some young women, particularly those such as Debbie and Sheila who had experienced problems in securing support from their families.

I did talk to my teacher, because I found out in the
six weeks holiday and I went back and told my
teacher, when I broke down with all the stress,
and coping on my own for a couple of months, it
took its toll. She was really good, do you know
what I mean, it's like she just wished I'd come to
her sooner, I'd left it about three weeks since
start of term, so she was very supportive and did
loads for me. (Debbie)

[The youth worker] were trying to do everything
she could to either get me away from me mum,
or get something sorted out about baby and that
but ... they didn't get owt sorted and too late
anyway 'cos me mum found out ... (Sheila)

Not all the young women experienced such support and one experienced a problem with her teachers.

Like one teacher said something to me and it
really upset me and he came and apologised and
said 'I didn't mean it to come like that, I were
trying to have a joke with you'. I said 'Yes but you
don't understand', and he said 'I know I don't',
and he were alright after that. (Barbara)

Another group who became involved in the pregnancy was health professionals. Here young women's expectations were low, leading to some of them avoiding contact as long as possible.

> *Well when I went to see my doctor I know I had been pregnant for ages, but I never went in to him until about three and half months. My doctor didn't ask me if I wanted to get rid of it, he just booked me in to see the midwife. He knew because I'd left it that long to go and see him in the first place so he just booked me in to see the midwife and didn't even ask me. He assumed.* (Rebecca)

This avoidance did not mean that in all cases the young women were themselves unaware of their pregnancy or had not disclosed it in their communities outside of family and close friends. Rather it was a deferment of what they saw as external interference and the critical judgements that health professionals might make about them as 'pregnant teenagers'. So, young women might for example have told their friends, their boyfriends, sisters or even parents, but still be unwilling to risk this judgement with their GP.

> *I got a definite attitude from the consultant he must have been in his 50s, ... his attitude was very much like stupid young mothers who don't know what they are doing, and don't know what they are getting themselves into.* (Cheryl)

> *One of the doctors I remember she said to me, when she heard how old I was she said 'Oh you'll have time for 30 kids you will the age you are'. I thought whatever.* (Moira)

This criticism was experienced as part of the abnormality of being a pregnant teenager and was also derived from certain members of their local communities with looks from 'older

people' and occasional name calling at school from other teenagers outside their immediate circle, during the pregnancy.

> *When I went to ante-natal classes for a check up, a lot of the women there were like, especially the older generation some of them looked at you, yet other older people would say 'Isn't he lovely' and they'd come up. So it depends it's not just age, there's a lot of middle class, middle aged people who look at you funny.* (Fiona)

> *You get funny looks when you go into shops where normal teenagers are, those that wouldn't do a thing wrong and they think they are better.* (Jane)

However such problems appeared to cease after the birth when the baby was integrated within the wider family. This may be to do with shifting perceptions of the pregnancy from a reflection of a young woman's irresponsible sexual activity, to a more acceptable phase of responsible motherhood. In many ways the young women themselves shared this view.

Comments

Young women are well aware, before they are faced with a possible pregnancy, of the beliefs, values, responses and levels of support that they can expect from their families and these expectations are usually fulfilled. Families and especially mothers can prove decisive in the integration of a teenage pregnancy into a family and its subsequent normalisation. Where problems with this normalisation process might occur, these are most likely to be with health professionals who are regarded both as being outside the local community due to their age or their professional standing and as likely to hold a generally critical attitude to teenage pregnancy; with older people in the community who are excluded due to age, or other teenagers whose experience differs to those of the pregnant teenager. Those immediately surrounding the young woman are most likely to offer support and welcome the new baby into the community after the initial shock.

7 Decision making and independence

When faced with the decision whether or not to continue with an unplanned pregnancy, young women are presented with a choice that can seem overwhelming. Moreover this is a decision where, because of its seriousness, others may be unwilling or unable to offer advice.

No not really it were my decision, it was up to me. They said 'It's your decision it's up to you and we'll stand by you whatever you do'. (Shelley)

I was crying when I first went to her, after my friend told my mum, and she said 'Don't cry it's done now, whatever you want to do I will stick by you. Give it a couple of days to think about it'. (Leone)

Thus, often for the first time, a young woman may suddenly find herself required to take the major responsibility for an important decision that will radically change her life. The information available to her in making this choice is often very limited, strong views might be expressed by her family, her boyfriend or her friends but these may be unhelpful in assisting the young woman achieve the right solution for her.

My friend Wendy she caught pregnant ... when she was 16 and had her when she was 17, she was only young ... she said ... 'I haven't got a life no more, if I could turn back clock no matter how much I love Elsie and everything I'd do things differently'. She said 'You are not going to have much of a life really'. My friend Amy left school at 15 because she was pregnant at school and when I used to see her she'd say 'It's the best thing in the world. It's going to be lovely for you'. So I had two differing opinions. I got right upset one night and walked out of house, I was trying to think how Iain felt and understand things from

his point of view and I was trying to understand what Wendy were saying, all of what they were saying, but nobody seemed to be listening to me, I was all mixed up and I think I was in shock. (Katrina)

For some the enormity of the decision may be too much and the issue of choice avoided completely by deferring to the preferences of others, either in choosing to continue or abort the pregnancy.

In other cases the decision may be deferred by not acknowledging the pregnancy at all.

I'd put it to the back of my mind. I convinced myself that I wasn't and I never could be. (Sally)

Of course deferment is itself likely to remove choice if it goes on for too long, leading to a birth as in the case of Sally whose pregnancy was not confirmed until she was five months pregnant.

However where a decision had to be made it was often the responsibility of the young woman alone, and one associated with prolonged periods of anxiety and stress.

Yes I used to cry myself to sleep every night thinking about it, but I just couldn't do it. I got to about three months and decided that I was keeping it. I told my mum I was keeping it and she is happy for me now. So everybody is happy for me now, it was just at first, a bit of a shock and that. (Rebecca)

In this way, unlike the young women's descriptions of early sexual encounters, pregnant young women claim to demonstrate adulthood in their terms by facing up to the consequences of their actions in having risky sex and subsequent conception. This is the case even if the circumstances of conception were out of their hands and the subsequent decision to continue with the pregnancy or not was in actuality a response to the expectations and limitations placed on them by others.

Continuing with the pregnancy and the transition to adulthood

It has been suggested that teenage pregnancy might represent one of the few remaining routes by which young people can achieve adulthood, involving as it does the creation of a new family unit with the possibility of independent living away from the family of origin. However this assertion has been disputed by the FPSC (1999) and others (Allen, 1998) who have argued that young women do not deliberately seek motherhood as a route to independent living. Moreover, on the evidence of our study, it would appear that whilst young women may leave the family home after the birth of their child, this was not the case in all families. Even where it was, the mother and child often continued to receive a considerable amount of support from her family. Whilst some of these young women were under 16 and therefore ineligible for social housing, even among those older there was often a preference for the continued support of their family, reflecting what we have called the early capture of the pregnancy.

Such a preference for continued family support suggests that for some young people teenage pregnancy might not represent a move away from the family but a re-integration within it at the same time as other teenagers might be forming their own identities outside the home. This capture of the pregnancy by the

extended family may result in a change in status for the young woman, but this change might be experienced more as a gradual moving away than a dramatic transition. Indeed, in the short term the pregnancy may be perceived by the young woman as heralding an increased state of dependency with a continuance of her reliance upon the wider family (Ruddick, 1993).

I think I coped really well but I've had my mum and dad there as well, so they are part of it. They have never took over they've just left me to look after him myself. But if I'd needed any advice or a little bit of help they've always been there to help me. (Sally)

She has him during the day all the time, and when I'm working, if I can't be bothered to get up in the morning she brings him down, and stuff like that. (Susie)

Other families adopted a more semi-dependent approach in their management of teenage pregnancy, choosing to continue to support their daughters in their own homes, either through child-minding or by offering continued financial support.

When I was at Mum's she will help me with money and buy him things, I don't like leaving him and I don't go out, so I don't need babysitters. She helps out a lot and my dad, they all help, they all beg to have him. (Cassey)

Well not financial really because Mark has got a job now and we're OK, but if I was feeling poorly, I would go to Mum's and she would look after Simon while I had a rest, or she'd have Simon overnight sometimes if I wanted to go out, or if I was feeling upset she'd be there for me really. Not really financially, more emotionally. (Moira)

What is likely is that in all families, even those resistant to the teenage pregnancy before birth, the new baby will be quickly integrated into the wider family network. This suggests that teenage motherhood may not be an automatic route into adulthood, rather part of a process of transition where notions of independence and dependence are negotiated: the young woman gradually learns to take responsibility for her child while her family seeks an appropriate level of intervention which might lead to a diminishment of reliance upon them.

> Q   Since you've been pregnant who has been the biggest source of support?
>
> S   Over the last two to three months it was my brother and his wife, because she'd had two kids. I think she was about 19 when she got pregnant. They were the most helpful near the end of the pregnancy. Then when I started getting close to somebody else they didn't like it, that's why we fell out. They were always trying to tell me what to do, who to be with. I was a mum. It was my decision what to do, nobody can tell me what to do, I don't have anything to do with them any more. (Tina)

This distancing may take place over a short period of time or it might be more protracted depending upon the relationship between the family and the young woman before the pregnancy and her living situation before the birth. For the four young mothers in our research who were not living with their families before they had their children, a transition had already taken place and this was seen as important in the ease with which their pregnancy was accepted by others and its contribution to their transition to adulthood.

> I think to be honest for a lot of teenage mums the problem is with people asking them, and the reason people didn't ask me was when I moved in with Julian I made a big decision and I proved to my parents and my friends I could live like an adult, choose my own paths and make my own decisions. I had to go to loggerheads with a lot of them to get that, and the fact I made my own decision the first time and proved them wrong, I think a lot of them didn't feel they could push their opinion on me. (Cheryl)

> I think it makes people grow up a lot more. Everybody told me I was really mature anyway but I think I've grown up a lot more since I've had [the baby]. I realise all about looking after kids, you've got to take responsibility for my own family, make sure they are well and I'm not going to go out and get into trouble, and get locked up and for my kids to go in a home. I think it keeps you out of trouble, it stops you from getting into a lot of mess. (Tina)

But such a change was not automatically a result of young motherhood. Not all young mothers wanted to leave their families of origin and set up home on their own.

Fatherhood and the transition to adulthood

In the focus groups with young men, young fatherhood was regarded as a particularly large step to take, principally because it involved becoming financially responsible for others, something to be avoided as long as possible. This was linked to notions of responsibility and masculinity within existing relationships before any pregnancy.

But 99 per cent of women, or 50 per cent of women are out there for money. I've had it done to me mesen, I've had somebody go out with me just for money. (Youth Club 2)

Women generally were seen as being motivated in their relationships by financial considerations and becoming pregnant was considered to be one route though which they could gain money.

Majority of single mums probably don't do it out of choice, but I think there'll be a fair few that aren't bothered, 'cos they're getting a house, and all, they're getting income support, what have you, they are not that badly off actually. (New Deal 5)

However this did not mean that they protected themselves from unwanted pregnancies, rather fatherhood was regarded as a somewhat inevitable transition route. For some this meant that there were advantages in going through fatherhood as soon as possible.

A *You're having a kid young, right, like, say I've got a kid now, at 15, ... I can be taking him things like, he might want to go to football every week ...*

B *You could go and work with your dad too at 15 and 13, know what I mean – it's not much difference.*

C *Well, kids round here, like, going out at 16 like to pubs and that, and having a dad who's not right older than him, it'd be* [someone] *for him to go out with.*

D *I'd love it if it were me!* (Youth club 2)

Not all young men were so keen to become fathers at a young age and this made them more willing to consider abortion.

Q *Would you want her to continue with the pregnancy?*

D *Yeah.*

B *No.*

V *I wouldn't – I'd ask her if she wanted an abortion.*

S *Depends how old I were – if she did, you can't do owt about it, I can't do nowt.* (New Deal 2)

For many, the expectation was that they would become fathers at some time, for some in the fairly near future.

W *You're about right age anyway to have a kid, ... 20.*

M *I bet I have a kid by time like, I'm 20, telling you way I go about.* (New Deal 1)

Having an abortion and the transition to adulthood

Like those who chose motherhood, the young women who chose not to continue with their pregnancies were also struck by the enormity of the decision facing them and in most cases had initially thought that they would continue with the pregnancy.

Q *And had you decided straight away what you were going to do?*

L *No. I were going to keep it, but, em, going to get rid of it.*

Q *What persuaded you?*

*L   Well, 'cos I'm too young and I want a job, and
     basically I would have nowhere to live, if I did
     keep it, you* [to mother] *said you wouldn't
     have me would you not with a baby.* (Lauren)

However, unlike those who chose to continue with their pregnancies most of these young women knew and had talked to other women who had had abortions.

*Q   And d'you know anyone else who's been
     pregnant?*

*A   Yeah. One of my best friends. And her friend.
     I know a lot of people.*

Q   And what've they done?

A   Got rid of it. (Jenny)

This appeared to allow the young woman to consider having an abortion, although like those choosing to continue there was some question as to whether or not the choice was entirely their own, with some young women having overt pressure put upon them (such as Lauren above whose mother had said she would have to leave home). Where the decision was identified by the young woman as not being her own, there was more regret shown, although still an appreciation that this might have been the best decision at the time.

*I did want to keep it, but I don't know. I think,
now, looking back, I still don't think what I did
was right 'cos I don't agree with abortion, but I
knew that, in the long term, it would be the right
thing that I did – 'cos now I'd be stuck at home
with a kid. With a three year old kid.* (Sheila)

For one young woman, in particular, who had her abortion some time ago, there was a change after making the decision and she found it hard to readjust to life as a teenager, despite her attempts.

*Then after a while I stopped crying and then I
went downstairs ... and I was alright and then I
went to KFC and to the pictures that night er
normal! Normal!* (Lisa)

This suggests that the decision to have an abortion may bring with it its own changes in the young woman concerned. Although it is difficult to make generalisations due to the small numbers in our sample and the immediacy of the abortion, in most cases, it does seem that during this brief period a young woman is involved in an often stressful and lonely balancing act: measuring her own and the surrounding community's dislike of abortion against her current needs and the opinions of those closest to her.

Comments

For both young women who choose to continue with their pregnancies and those who do not, this decision-making process can be a traumatic one, that can bring about change irrespective of the decision made. However if the decision is to continue with the pregnancy, the mediation of others in managing this outcome will help the young woman live with her choice and to negotiate the difficult move into motherhood. But the immediate effect of this help may also be in keeping young mothers dependent on their families of origin and preventing them making the transition to adulthood in the same way as other teenagers. They may, for example, not risk the rigours of trying to leave the family home because they can rely upon their parents.

For young women who elect to have an

abortion a similar process of decision making takes place. However, these young women will also have to negotiate the views of their wider community and in particular anti-abortion opinions of others. Like those who decide to keep their babies, in order to do this they need the support and experiences of others.

For young men, the responsibility for supporting a new family is often seen as theirs alone, and in this respect fatherhood can be regarded as more of a route to adulthood than motherhood. This was especially so in those areas where economic independence was hardest to achieve.

8   The period of decision making

Teenage pregnancy is regarded as problematic because of the age of the mother and the consequences of this for both herself and any subsequent children (NHS Centre for Reviews and Dissemination, 1997). This is in stark contrast to the majority of pregnancies that occur to older women who, whilst occasionally faced with a problematic pregnancy, are nevertheless thought to be able to cope with motherhood.

Where pregnancies are regarded as problematic, this can be at a personal level or in terms of a wider society. At the personal level, there may be a number of contingent factors (to do with an individual's personal health or immediate family circumstances, for example) which may mean that a particular pregnancy causes specific difficulties. This may be true for women from a variety of social backgrounds. Pregnancy becomes *socially* problematic when it is regarded as creating additional problems at a wider societal level; where, for example, it is seen to be related to the specific circumstances of social exclusion that individuals, social groups or wider communities may experience.

Teenage pregnancy falls within this second category. Higher teenage birth rates are correlated with regional and economic patterns, being higher in northern than southern regions and in primary compared with service sector occupations. Moreover, young women from deprived areas are up to six times more likely to choose to follow pregnancy through to birth than teenage young women in affluent areas (FPSC, 1999).

These rates are also shaped by wider social trends, such as changing household and marital patterns that may be thought to contribute to the 'problem'. Thus:

- in 1981, 55 per cent of live births to teenagers took place in marriage

- in 1997, only 11 per cent of live births to teenagers occurred within marriage.

It is clear that when considering specific statistics (for different regions, for example) or more general social patterns, there is a presumption that reproduction is most appropriate at a particular stage of the life course when stable economic, household and personal relationships are in place.

Given this, we have found it useful to consider the data from this project in terms of the ways in which teenage pregnancy is constructed, and experienced, as problematic and the impact this has on the decisions available and those chosen. By comparing the accounts of the young women (and others) we talked to against other studies of 'normal' reproduction, we looked at how the pregnancy was different for these young women and what led them to make the decision they did.

Comparing adult and teenage pregnancy

One of the key themes emerging from this project is that even when teenage pregnancy is prevalent, and widely discussed compared to abortion, work still has to be done by the young woman along with her immediate family to normalise it. We need to ask whether this process of normalisation mirrors in any way the experiences of those women who have an 'adult' pregnancy and subsequently what in this process of normalisation is influential on the decision made. Studies of pregnant women (McMahon, 1995; Bailey, 1999) have tended to focus on those who are partnered, aged 23 to 30, middle class and normally working in the service sector. For these women faced with a pregnancy, certain key characteristics are instrumental in the decision to become mothers, and we can compare these with the experiences of the teenage mothers in our study. Each of the bullet points below summarises the experience of women going through pregnancy as 'normal', and each is followed by comment on how this does or does not apply to teenage mothers.

- Motherhood confirms a woman's status as 'adult', making it an important 'rite of passage' for women.

  Unlike normal pregnancy, the relationship between motherhood and its conferring of adult status for teenagers is much more problematic. On the one hand, among teenage (actual and prospective) mothers we did find evidence of a strong sense of personal responsibility and self-determination which was linked to claims to the adult status that they made.

  On the other hand, in many cases they experienced a wide dependency on their family for support, both during the pregnancy and afterwards. Of course, older women living in close proximity to their families might experience similar support but given the focus of this research we have no evidence to support this.

  In addition, other adults – for example, in ante-natal clinics, midwifery, and social services staff – do not treat them as 'adults' with the levels of social competency and autonomy that would presume.

- Whether planned or not, the identity of motherhood in 'normal' pregnancy is actively chosen with a powerful discourse about the maternal role and its responsibilities developing early in the pregnancy.

  Among our respondents, this discourse was also found, and was illustrated in a number of ways:
  - in the way most did not see abortion as an option
  - in the sense of responsibility (i.e. culpability) for the pregnancy mixed with a different sense of responsibility for (i.e. looking after) the child
  - this second sense was also seen by the respondents to be one reason why abortion *might* be considered acceptable if another pregnancy came along.

  What is particularly interesting is that motherhood becomes an important consideration mostly after their decision to see through the pregnancy to full term; elsewhere they speak of the shock and fear they experienced when discovering they were pregnant. It would seem that for teenage mothers claims to responsibility are constructed during the pregnancy. These may involve considerably more negotiation work on the part of the pregnant teenager than the 'normal' mother, who may have considered herself open to conception before it occurs.

- Normal pregnancy changes the previous sense of self.

Studies of adult pregnancy suggest that it is normalised as a break with a previous sense of self with the woman constructing a positive new dimension to the self through motherhood. For teenage mothers, this is more problematic.

Our focus groups with non-pregnant young women demonstrated the negotiation of self and identity that takes place during the teenage years in association with peers. Teenage pregnancy removes young women from their peers. This suggests that in contrast to normal pregnancy, there is much more of a break with, than a sense of adding a new dimension to, the previous sense of self. Teenage mothers may find it difficult to maintain links with friends or to make friends with other mothers unless they too are young. This suggests that teenage mothers might represent a distinct group divorced from both other teenagers and other (adult) mothers.

- Changes in body shape also reshape personal identity in part because of the way people respond to the pregnant woman through her physical changes.

It is clear that the young women in our study experienced a similar process of becoming pregnant after the decision to continue was made and the pregnancy became more apparent. However, for young mothers this process was part of the capture of their pregnancy by their wider family and the pregnancy becoming normalised, after the decision to continue was made and the birth came closer.

This was different to their earlier experiences of pregnancy when they were faced with the private information provided by their bodies – the missed period etc. – and had a private sense of whether they were 'really' pregnant (despite tests to the contrary given by health agencies), which was gradually disclosed to others.

- Adult pregnancy has been presented as a legitimate excuse to withdraw from work, and take up motherhood as a full-time job accompanied by worries about the impact the pregnancy will have on the mother's claims to professional status in the workplace, and her ability to return to work.

For the young women we talked to, anxieties were expressed about the impact of pregnancy on schooling and work, and some made efforts or intended to retrieve their school career subsequently. However, because of the way the pregnancy tended to be integrated within the existing family, motherhood was not automatically viewed as a full-time job. Young women often had to make a subsequent decision to take childcare duties away from their mothers. There was also less of a sense of the notion that pregnancy offers a 'return' to a private space since the young women often remained dependent on their family of origin.

The decision-making process

This last point highlights the impact of other people in capturing and defining the pregnancy, thereby shaping the decision to continue with it or not. In considering all the aspects of the acquisition of motherhood described above, it is important to recognise that the decision is not a once and for all event or moment that can be found in each of the teenager's accounts. On the contrary, decision making and choosing to follow through with a pregnancy is a complex and multi-layered process that depends on interaction with parents, boyfriends, peers and wider community from well before a pregnancy is confirmed. In this respect a teenage pregnancy is far more of a socially negotiated event than a 'normal' pregnancy.

In Figure 3 we have tried to represent the key stages and related factors that shape the decision-making process during the period of the ('abnormal') teenage pregnancy compared with a 'normal' pregnancy. It should be noted that many decisions may be unchallengeable by this time.

There are a number of elements in Figure 3 worth further comment. First, we should note that the discovery of the pregnancy was not necessarily straightforward: often it required repeat tests that may include false negatives: 'am I or am I not pregnant' caused considerable anxiety and insecurity for a number of our respondents.

Second, the dependency on others means that the definition of the pregnancy as normal or not is not something which the teenage girl has complete control over, unlike the 'normal' pregnancy.

Third, there are various outcomes relating to 'normalisation' of a new identity – as the third stage on the figure suggests – some involving abortion, others full-term delivery. We can note that at this stage, there can be a divergence between mother/adult statuses for the 'abnormal' teenage pregnancy compared with the 'normal' adult pregnancy.

Comments

This comparison shows that for both 'normal' (adult) and 'abnormal' (teenage) pregnancy there are important points during the course of the pregnancy which require decisions to be made. It also shows, however, that the decision-making process for young women is made more problematic by the partial capture of the pregnancy and so its definition by significant others. The 'choice' to continue with or terminate a pregnancy is a decision that firms up in the period between seven and 14 weeks: the key time is that between the discovery of pregnancy – usually after the missed second period – and the subsequent two months when the teenage girl must confront and negotiate various options and routes which might lead to full-term delivery or termination. Presumably – though there are no secondary sources of data to confirm this – adult women who discover they have an unplanned pregnancy also have to go through a difficult period when decisions must be made; yet, we would expect there to be much greater control in determining courses of action here, compared with the teenager.

This comparison clearly needs to be treated carefully as it is based on assumptions about 'normal' pregnancy, albeit supported by empirical secondary research. These assumptions, one should add, are also tied to the experience of a white Anglo-Saxon culture:

Figure 3   Decision making as a process: comparing normal and teenage pregnancy

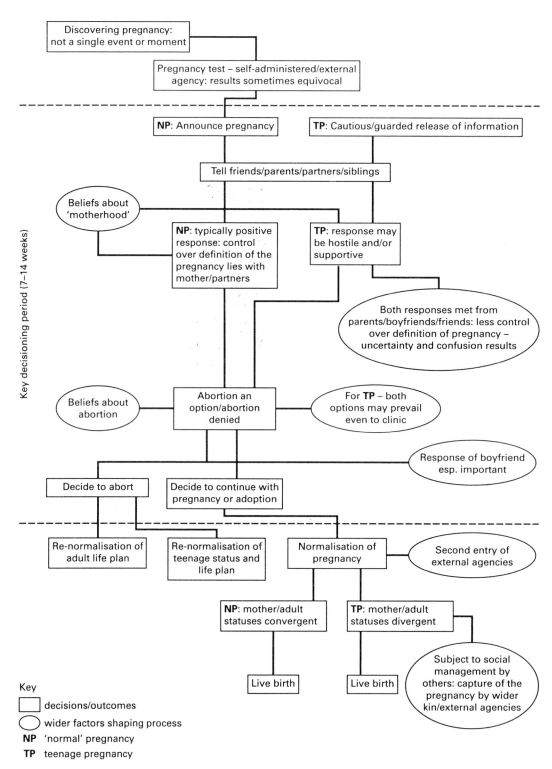

Key decisioning period (7–14 weeks)

Discovering pregnancy: not a single event or moment

Pregnancy test – self-administered/external agency: results sometimes equivocal

NP: Announce pregnancy

TP: Cautious/guarded release of information

Tell friends/parents/partners/siblings

Beliefs about 'motherhood'

NP: typically positive response: control over definition of the pregnancy lies with mother/partners

TP: response may be hostile and/or supportive

Both responses met from parents/boyfriends/friends: less control over definition of pregnancy – uncertainty and confusion results

Beliefs about abortion

Abortion an option/abortion denied

For **TP** – both options may prevail even to clinic

Response of boyfriend esp. important

Decide to abort

Decide to continue with pregnancy or adoption

Re-normalisation of adult life plan

Re-normalisation of teenage status and life plan

Normalisation of pregnancy

Second entry of external agencies

NP: mother/adult statuses convergent

TP: mother/adult statuses divergent

Subject to social management by others: capture of the pregnancy by wider kin/external agencies

Live birth

Live birth

Key

☐   decisions/outcomes

◯   wider factors shaping process

NP   'normal' pregnancy

TP   teenage pregnancy

there is in that regard much more work to be done exploring women's experiences of pregnancy among different ethnic communities, for both teenage and adult members thereof. Nevertheless, as we shall see in Chapter 9, there are some important policy implications that emerge from this close inspection of pregnancy choices and decision making within the communities of Doncaster that we surveyed, and which have wider applicability elsewhere in the UK.

9 Implications for policy

What policy implications might arise from this examination of the decision making that frames teenage pregnancies from before conception, through the immediate post-conception period to birth?

Before conception

The findings here appear to support the results of those few studies that have examined in detail young people's experiences of sex education in the UK. That is, that it has little real relevance to the context in which sexuality is experienced, and, as importantly, that it tends to be given in such a way as to protect the young from exposure to 'too much' sexual knowledge. As West (1999) has observed, the dominant sex education model in the UK is 'to shield [the young] from sexual knowledge that might corrupt their innocence'. As it currently stands, sex education in the UK appears not to protect a significant number of young people from unplanned teenage conceptions.

We need to look very carefully at the ways in which this lack of protection may be doubly compounded by a further exclusion – the absence of, severely truncated or one-sided discussion of abortion in sex education agendas – which can effectively block a second opportunity for informed choice in the decision to go ahead or not with an unplanned pregnancy. West also goes on to note that 'the greater acceptance of young people's sexuality in the Netherlands (and Sweden) than the UK may reflect a higher, more independent status for the young as much as a generally more open climate around sexuality' (p. 70). An acceptance of sexuality and regard for independence imply that young people are capable of making fully informed decisions about crucial issues in the light of all the available facts, including access to informed, unbiased and sensitive discussion of abortion. This may also in part explain why both the Dutch teenage conception and birth rates are so much lower than in the UK.

West's remarks also suggest that where more young people are given support as independent (young) adults, the transition to adulthood which some – not all – seek through pregnancy, may be achieved via other means.

There are also a number of specific points arising from this project that directly relate to the experiences of young people.

- Most teenagers said they gained their sex education through friends, magazines and television. In view of this there is a need to consider how these media might be better exploited both in and out of school as suggested within the SEU's *Teenage Pregnancy* report.

- Contraceptive services were seen as inaccessible or unacceptable because of concerns about confidentiality and attitudes. Young men rarely saw clinics as somewhere they would go themselves. This suggests a need to develop appropriate services and to overcome any perceived barriers.

- Abortion was not considered as a positive option, by both young women and young men, and often not considered at all. In order to broaden understanding among young people about the choices that they might face, the research suggests that more discussion is needed on this issue.

- Young mothers were often shocked by the

amount of time and effort involved in looking after a baby; more needs to be done to advise young women and men on the demands of parenthood and its incompatibility with the demands of being a teenager.

- Parental and community values about motherhood and abortions were regarded as very important factors in decision making, particularly with respect to the negative associations that abortion has. Parents and community should be informed about the options open to young people, and involved in discussion about strategy and provision.

- The relationship of young men to fatherhood was especially complex: most saw fatherhood as indicating a transition to adulthood based upon their assumption of economic responsibility for the child. This was not, however, linked to taking responsibility in their relationship for contraception itself. Engaging with young men and involving them in the issues are clearly areas that need addressing.

The decision-making period

The data show the importance of the period between discovery of pregnancy and the decision to pursue the pregnancy to full term. There are a number of key practical implications suggested by the research.

- It suggests a possible target period for counselling/advice and intervention, which is during the seven to 14 week period of the pregnancy. This extends the potential time for intervention and management of teenage pregnancy into the post-conception period. Whilst the *Teenage Pregnancy* report (Social Exclusion Unit, 1999) recommends greater provision for advice during early pregnancy, we demonstrate that the timing and nature of the advice offered is crucial. Our provision points to the sort of strategy to adopt.

- Counselling/advice during this period should be particularly attentive to the likely sources of existing influence relating to wider beliefs, the nature of relationships, the circumstances in which the pregnancy originated, and the patterns of 'capture' of the pregnancy by significant others.

- Counselling/advice services need also to be aware that the period of possible advice/intervention may be very brief, potential recipients hard to reach, and key decisions made very early in a pregnancy.

- It suggests ways in which wider problems – of deprivation and social exclusion – are mediated at the personal/interpersonal level. This helps to explain why, within a population of similar socio-economic status and resource, it is some, rather than all, teenage pregnancies that go to full term.

- It suggests that a mixture of general approaches together with targeted counselling and support might make it possible to present abortion as a genuine option from pre-conception onwards.

- It could point to ways in which external agencies might develop new approaches to the wider social management of pregnancy, through opening up more debate between agencies about the range of options that are open to young women, and their implications.

Birth and afterwards

One of the main influences found to affect the decision to continue or terminate a pregnancy is the way in which parents and the wider extended family accommodate and indeed even embrace the pregnancy. Such a 'capturing' of the pregnancy was found to be instrumental in normalising the pregnancy, both within the family and within the wider community. This clearly has important implications for policy initiatives such as the government's Sure Start Plus programme, since it can be hypothesised that the process of 'capture' will vary according to different family structures and family relations. The extent of this capture will play an important role in determining the type and amount of family support available and consequent levels of need for, or recruitment into, supported housing.

Yet little or nothing is known about this relationship between capture, familial relations and patterns of support that might be expected by and actually given to young (teenage) mothers (and their partners). It can be hypothesised that much may depend on the way families negotiate the boundaries of familial relationships around the transition to adulthood, particularly with regard to claims to autonomy teenagers make and the ability or willingness of their parents to respond to these claims (Brannen, 1994). In particular the assumption that it is 'families' who will carry the burden of the new baby in practice often revolved around the support offered by the mothers of the pregnant teenager. The mother played a key mediating role within the family in two ways. First, she negotiated the acceptance of the daughter's pregnancy with her often more negative and hostile husband. Second, she offered emotional, practical and financial support during the pregnancy and after the birth of the baby. As presented in the study, without this support many pregnant teenagers may well have made very different decisions about their pregnancy. This is particularly the case where the relationship to the father of the baby was not well established or had already ended.

An important research task, therefore, is to explore the dynamics of boundary negotiation, pregnancy capture and its normalisation across different types of family, different familial relationships and different classes. The role and situation of mothers of pregnant teenagers, as they offer a form of 'partnership parenthood' with their daughters, and how this develops and evolves once the child is born, looks of particular interest.

10 Conclusions

The current government initiatives in the area of teenage pregnancy have rightly included a call for more research and data collection that can help explain why teenage conception and pregnancy rates remain high in the UK, compared with other countries. Much of the likely answer will lie in improved educational and occupational opportunity for those in deprived areas, as well as better information and advice on accessing family planning clinics. Moreover, it is likely that the more differentiated the approach – to meet the different needs of young people found in a variety of social settings (including, for example, those in care; see Corlyon and McGuire, 1997) – the better the chance of success.

We found little evidence in our data of young women actively seeking pregnancy as a route to adulthood. On the contrary, pregnancy often reconfirmed, though in new ways, dependency relations within the family and partnerships, particularly in mother/daughter relationships. As we argued, teenage pregnancy might not represent a move away from the family into 'adulthood' but a reintegration within it. Paradoxically, while she stays at home the teenage mother may have both more and less independence. She gives some of her autonomy over the child to the family, especially to her own mother. Because of this, she shares the standard of living of the household, may be freed to work, continue at school and have a fuller social life, but she will rarely be able to provide financially for herself and her child. However, leaving the family home often means that she has fewer possibilities for work, study or a social life, and little money at the same time as other teenagers are establishing their own identities outside the home.

We also found that most young women chose to continue with or end their pregnancy over a key period of time during which various routes – and their implications – were explored, often in difficult and confusing circumstances. These 'routes' were chosen in light of anticipations or expectations the teenagers had, which, of course, will in turn depend on local circumstances – whether there is a shared sense of the outcome of a particular decision and how far this is likely to be reinforced among friends and the wider community. While expectations about the impact of the arrival of a child do form part of a shared local culture, we found little or no evidence that people discussed or shared social knowledge about abortion among those we interviewed. Policy interventions should not unintentionally reinforce this position, even if there is no desire to encourage higher levels of abortion among young women.

Policy should also recognise the different conceptions and experiences of the life course for younger people in disadvantaged communities such as Doncaster. It was clear from interviews and focus groups that maturity and claims to social competency arrive much earlier here than is often seen to be the norm, while the young men's view was often that any parenting responsibilities towards their own children would probably be complete by their mid-20s. Thus, there may be quite different time-frames that circulate in particular community cultures, which help to normalise younger pregnancies.

If so, sex education is clearly addressing only a part of the wider social dynamic that reproduces higher levels of teenage pregnancy than outside Britain. However, we do not want to overplay the role of local cultures since the statistical evidence shows that the majority of young teenagers in areas of deprivation do not become pregnant and that more prosperous areas also have higher levels of pregnancy than our European neighbours. The research here stresses instead the combination of factors that can come into play after conception is discovered and the contingencies as well as patterns of choice that they prompt. In this regard, a new focus on the post-conception period should encourage a new approach to counselling which may, in the longer term, help to reduce overall levels of teenage pregnancy. It could do so through providing more informed advice to young people, parents and the wider community about the challenges, difficulties and uncertainties that the discovery of pregnancy will bring. This would help to foster a more realistic understanding of the impact of pregnancy on the routes to adulthood that are open to young people.

References

Abortion Law Reform Association (1997) *A Report on NHS Abortion Services*. London: ALRA

Allen, I. (1998) *Teenage Mothers: Decisions and Outcomes*. London: Policy Studies Institute

Bailey, L. (1999) 'Refracted selves? A study in changes in self-identity in the transition to motherhood', *Sociology*, Vol. 33, No. 3, pp. 335–52

Brannen, J. (1994) *Young People, Health and Family Life*. Milton Keynes: Open University

Burges, L. and Brown, M. (1995) *Single Lone Mothers*. London: Family Studies Centre

Corlyon, J. and McGuire, C. (1997) *Young Parents in Public Care*. London: National Children's Bureau

Fleissig, A. (1991) 'Unintended pregnancies and the use of contraception: changes from 1984 to 1989', *British Medical Journal*, Vol. 302, p. 147

FPSC (1999) *Teenage Pregnancy and the Family*, Family Briefing Paper 9. London: FPSC

Fritz, H. and Kitzinger, C. (1998) '"Emotion work" as a participant resource: a feminist analysis of young women's talk in interaction', *Sociology*, Vol. 32, No. 2, pp. 299–320

Furstenberg, F. (1987) *Adolescent Mothers in Later Life*. Cambridge: Cambridge University Press

Hawkes, G. (1995) 'Responsibility and irresponsibility: family planning', *Sociology*, Vol. 29, No. 2, pp. 257–73

Health Education Authority (1999) *Young People's Experiences of Relationships, Sex and Early Parenthood: Qualitative Research*. London: Health Education Authority

Holland, J., Ramazanoglu, C., Scott, S., Sharpe, S. and Thomson, R. (1990a) *'Don't Die of Ignorance', I Nearly Died of Embarrassment: Condoms in Context*. London: The Tufnell Press

Holland, J., Ramazanoglu, C. and Scott, S. (1990b) *Sex, Risk and Danger: Aids Education Policy and Young Women's Sexuality*. London: The Tufnell Press

Holland, J., Ramazanoglu, C., Sharpe, S. and Thomson, R. (1991) *Pressured Pleasure: Young Women and the Negotiation of Sexual Boundaries*. London: The Tufnell Press

Jones, G. (1995) *Family Support for Young People*. London: Family Studies Centre

McMahon, M. (1995) *Engendering Motherhood: Identity and Self-transformation in Women's Lives*. New York: Guildford Press

Metson, D. (1991) 'Lessons from an audit of unplanned pregnancies', *British Medical Journal*, Vol. 297, pp. 904–6

Moore, S. and Rosenthal, D. (1993) *Sexuality in Adolescence*. London: Routledge

NHS Centre for Reviews and Dissemination (1997) 'Preventing and reducing the effects of unplanned teenage pregnancies', *Effective Health Care Bulletin*, Vol. 3, No. 1, pp. 1–12

Office for National Statistics (1997) *Population Trends 88*. London: The Stationery Office

Office of National Statistics (1998) *1997 Birth Statistics, Series FM1*. London: Office of National Statistics

Phoenix, A. (1991) *Young Mothers?* Oxford: Blackwell

Prendergast, S. and Forrest, S. (1997) 'Hieroglyphs of the heterosexual: learning about gender in school', in L. Segal (ed.) *New Sexual Agendas*. London: Macmillan

Ruddick, S. (1993) 'Procreative choice for adolescent women', in A. Lawson and D. Rhode (eds.) *The Politics of Pregnancy: Adolescent Sexuality and Public Policy*. New Haven and London: Yale University Press

Social Exclusion Unit (1999) *Teenage Pregnancy*, Cm 4342. London: The Stationery Office

Thomson, R. and Scott, S. (1991) *Learning About Sex: Young Women and the Social Construction of Sexual Identity*. London: The Tufnell Press

West, J. (1999) '(Not) talking about sex', *Sociological Review*, Vol. 47, August, pp. 525–47